C000284075

HAMPSHIRE
NARROW GAUGE
including the Isle of Wight

Vic Mitchell and Keith Smith

MP Middleton Press

Cover pictures:
Front upper - Dean Hill (P. Nicholson)
Front lower - Exbury Gardens (R.Rundle)
Rear upper - Hythe Pier (P.G.Barnes)
Rear lower - East Hayling (J.H.Meredith)

Published July 2004

ISBN 1 904474 36 5

© Middleton Press, 2004

Design David Pede

Published by
        Middleton Press
        Easebourne Lane
        Midhurst, West Sussex
        GU29 9AZ
Tel: 01730 813169
Fax: 01730 812601
Email: info@middletonpress.co.uk
www.middletonpress.co.uk

Printed & bound by Biddles Ltd, Kings Lynn

CONTENTS

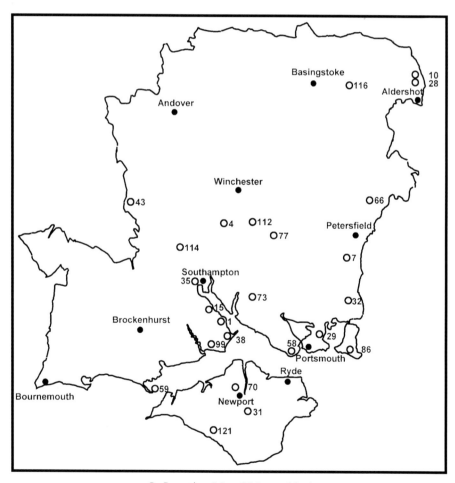

I. Location Map (N.Langridge)

INTRODUCTION

We have had to omit many of the minor lines, such as those used at the watercress beds which were established on the streams emanating from the Chalk mass that forms the northern part of Hampshire. Along its southern border were a number of gravel carrying lines, notably at Fawley, Marchwood, Nursling and Totton.

Seldom seen was a 3ft 1⅛ ins gauge line in a two mile long tunnel under Southampton Water, this carrying power cables from generators at Fawley. A battery-electric vehicle operated this maintenance railway in the 1970s.

Two Hampshire gasworks had railways. Hilsea had Bagnall 0-4-2Ts on 2ft 6ins track, while Winnal (north of Winchester) had a 2ft 8ins overhead - electric powered system.

The Navy seems to have used rail transport for munitions at Priddy's Hard from about 1850. By 1900, there were two lines (1ft 6ins and 2ft 6ins), the latter eventually superseding the former. Eight battery-electric locomotives arrived in 1929-30 and the system lasted until about 1960.

Another Naval line was laid down adjacent to the former Stokes Bay branch soon after its acquisition in 1922. The Royal Engineers had a line in this vicinity from the 1880s to about 1919, with two Hunslet 4-6-0Ts for motive power. There is also evidence of a wind powered sail trolley being used.

Members of the Isle of Wight Steam Railway compiled notes on many of the Island lines as follows:

Alverstone Brickworks, Whippingham. Nothing known other than that it existed and is shown on the pre-war OS maps.

Atherfield, Barnes High. It operated approximately 1928 to 1939 and connected a cliff top sandpit to the road.

Atherfield, B.J.Newnham & Sons. A rope-worked incline was in operation from about 1948 to the early 1950s when gale damage destroyed much of the equipment. It used to haul shingle up the cliff. A Fordson tractor was also used.

Atherfield, Sutton Cliff. Rope-hauled, single track incline for removing shingle from the beach. Turntable and temporary tracks along the beach. In use from about 1928 to about 1939.

Blackwater Incline. A cable-worked incline from St. George's Down to the Newport-Arreton road near the junction with the Blackwater road. Gauge about 2ft; originally single line, passing loop installed later. Also feeder lines at top of incline.

Bleak Down Gravel Pits. Extensive system connecting pits to a washing and crushing plant. Skips moved by hand or horses. Gauge not known.

Bouldnor. Horse-drawn tramway connecting a brickworks to two jetties.

Brading Brickworks. Small tramway about 50yds long and with about four skips.

Cement Works, Newport.
    (a) Main tramway system of 1ft. 7½ ins gauge had a petrol locomotive.
    (b) 3ft. 6ins gauge in pit for a chain-driven scoop.
    (c) Isolated section of 2ft. 11ins gauge - purpose not known.
    (d) Isolated section of 15¾ ins gauge - purpose not known.

Cowes Gasworks. The 1907 OS map shows two lines serving a jetty and the retort houses.

Downend Lime Quarry. The 1939 OS map shows a single line running from east to west.

Folly Works, Whippingham. A 2ft gauge tramway served a works and jetty using a Lister petrol engine. Built in WWI and scrapped about 1956.

Fort Victoria, Yarmouth. One system joining the pier with the fort and another 18ins system within the fort. It is not known whether the two systems joined.

Gunville Brickworks. Maps show what appears to be a short tramway from the pit to the works. Production began in the 1850s and ceased in the 1940s.

Hamstead House. This was the first railway to be built on the Island and it opened in 1832. There were two lines, each with passing loops, between Hamstead House and Farm to a quay on Newtown River. Malleable iron bars were laid in chairs on stone sleepers and horses hauled the "chaudrons".

Hansen & Co. East Cowes. 150yd long tramway connecting this firm's works to a jetty and crossing Castle Street.

Hillis Brickworks. This possessed a small tramway system with one hopper.

Kingston Generating Station, East Cowes. A 170yd tramway ran in a straight line from the jetty to the building. Possibly only used in constructing the station.

Lee Brickworks. Short tramway between pit and kilns shown in OS maps. It was west of Newport.

Liquid Fuel Engineering Co. East Cowes. A tramway connected the works with their water frontage, crossing Medina Road (now obliterated by Columbine Works).

Newport Sewage Works. Temporary tramroad believed to have been laid to bring materials in when the new works at Fairlee was built in about 1936.

Robin Hill. This nature park occupies a site formerly used by an old brickworks and remains of a tramway have been found there.

Royal National Hospital, Ventnor. A 2ft 6ins gauge tramway was used in a tunnel for hand-propelled rubbish skips.

Ryde Gasworks. A 2ft 3ins cable hauled tramway ran on elevated track from the retort house to the yard.

Ryde Railway Works. Narrow gauge rails crossed the running rails in the works at right-angles and were used for hand-propelled trolleys carrying heavy equipment. The rails once ran outside the works as well.

St.Helens Gasworks. 1ft 11½ ins gauge system crossed a road to connect the gasworks with the standard gauge sidings at St. Helens Quay.

Shamblers Brickworks, Cowes. A tramway of about 150 yds ran eastwards from the kilns to a jetty. The Cowes & Newport Railway had to build a bridge over it.

Shide Quarry. As well as the standard gauge sidings, there was a 20ins gauge system.

Steephill Quarry, Ventnor. Situated about a quarter of a mile from Ventnor Town Station (and served by a standard gauge siding), it had about 165yds of tramway.

Sunnycrest Nurseries, Newchurch. Length was about 200yds and it was hand-powered with two skips.

Upton Cross Brickworks.
    (a) 1ft 11½ ins gauge system.
    (b) 15 ins gauge part-elevated system running to a stone crushing plant.

Ventnor Gasworks. Little known other than that a tramway existed.

Ventnor Harbour. Used in the construction of the harbour and East Pier. There appears to have been more than one gauge in use. A picture of the foundering of the PS Chancellor in 1863 shows some of the tracks and trucks in the foreground.

J.S.White's Shipyards, Cowes & East Cowes.
    A tramway ran round all the shops at Cowes and there were steam cranes at Cowes and East Cowes.

    The maps are to the scale of 25 ins to 1 mile with north at the top, unless otherwise indicated.

    We are very grateful for the assistance received from many of the photographers and also from D. Allenby, E.W.Crawforth, B.Curl, H.Davies, B.Gent, R.Griffiths, P.Hitchcock, P.Keat (Gosport Railway Society coll.), Sarah Marsden, P.Marshman, C.Morgan, L.Munckton, M.Petch, Mrs J.Reilly, Mr D. & Dr S.Salter, I.Wilson and, as always, our wives Barbara Mitchell and Janet Smith.

Vic Mitchell Keith Smith
June 2004

1. Commercial
AGWI REFINERY, FAWLEY

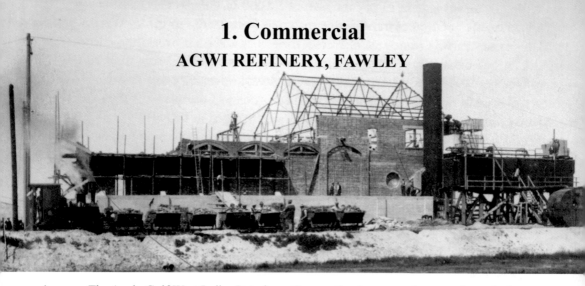

1.	The Anglo Gulf West Indies Petroleum Corporation began work on a refinery in August 1920 and, owing to the inadequacies of local roads, most materials were conveyed by water to a new quay in Ashlett Creek. From here, a two-foot gauge network was constructed. A Decauville 0-4-0T was recorded during construction of the power station. Esso took over later. (Esso Petroleum)

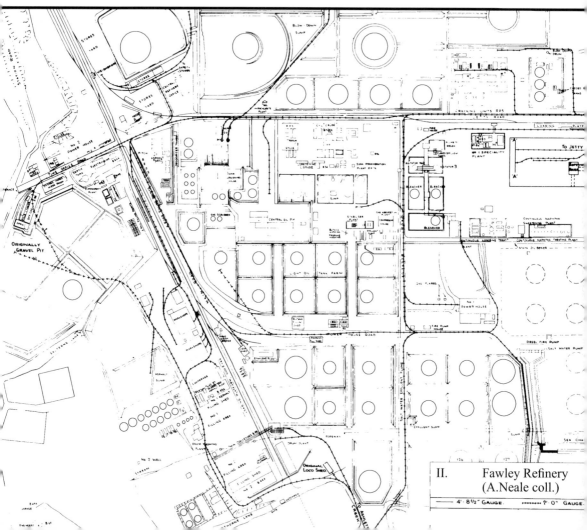

II.	Fawley Refinery
(A.Neale coll.)

4' 8½" GAUGE.　　　　2' 0" GAUGE

2.　　The refinery came into use on 18th June 1921, but was not connected to the Southern Railway until 1925 - see our *Southampton to Bournemouth* album. An asphalt plant was completed by 1924 and this generated up to 150 tons daily for conveyance to the jetty. Motor Rail no. H13 arrived in 1927, the fourth in the fleet. Four more came in 1928 and a further three in 1936-39. Surprisingly, two steam locomotives were used initially. (Esso Petroleum)

3.　　No. H13 is seen with a loaded train, while empty drums pass overhead. A 30-minute interval service was operated for workers initially, but it was gradually reduced to "as required" after 1945. Also conveyed were refinery components, coke, acid tar, hypochloride, caustic soda and fire-fighting equipment. The line was little used after 1957 and no. H17 was presented to the Hampshire Narrow Gauge Railway Society on 1st November 1961. (Esso Petroleum)

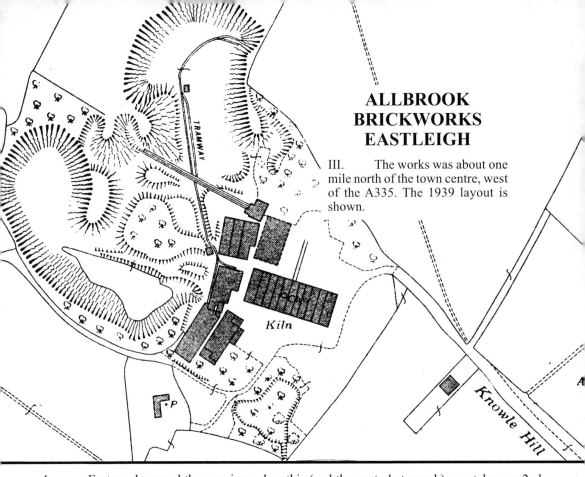

ALLBROOK BRICKWORKS EASTLEIGH

III.   The works was about one mile north of the town centre, west of the A335. The 1939 layout is shown.

TRAMWAY

Kiln

Knowle Hill

4.   Eastwoods owned the premises when this (and the next photograph) was taken on 2nd August 1964. This loading ramp allowed transfer of clay to road vehicles. (C.G.Down)

5.	This is the rear view of Motor Rail no. 8687 at the tipping shed. Note the choice of coupling height. (C.G.Down)

6.	An August 1968 photograph shows Motor Rail no. 5862 of 1934 at the fuel tank. By that time the works was in the ownership of Redland Bricks Ltd. (P.Nicholson)

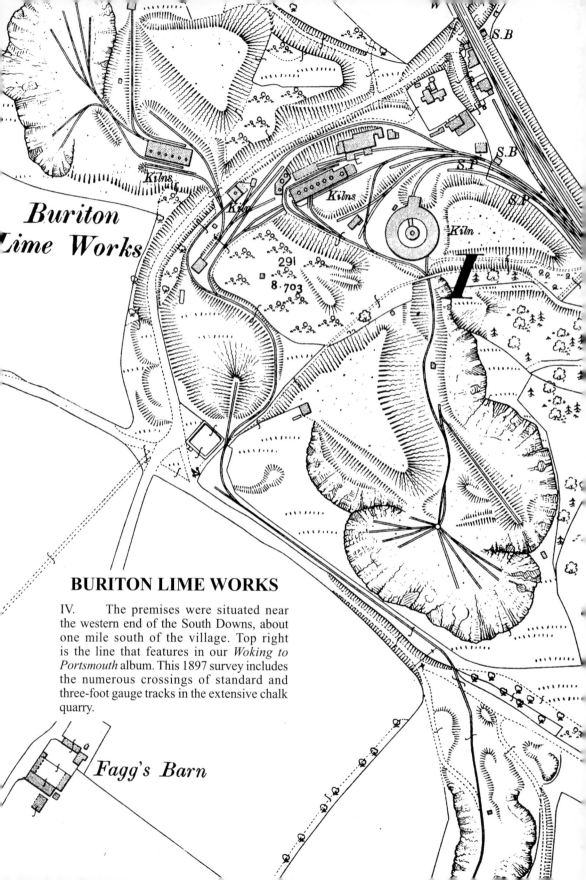

BURITON LIME WORKS

IV.   The premises were situated near the western end of the South Downs, about one mile south of the village. Top right is the line that features in our *Woking to Portsmouth* album. This 1897 survey includes the numerous crossings of standard and three-foot gauge tracks in the extensive chalk quarry.

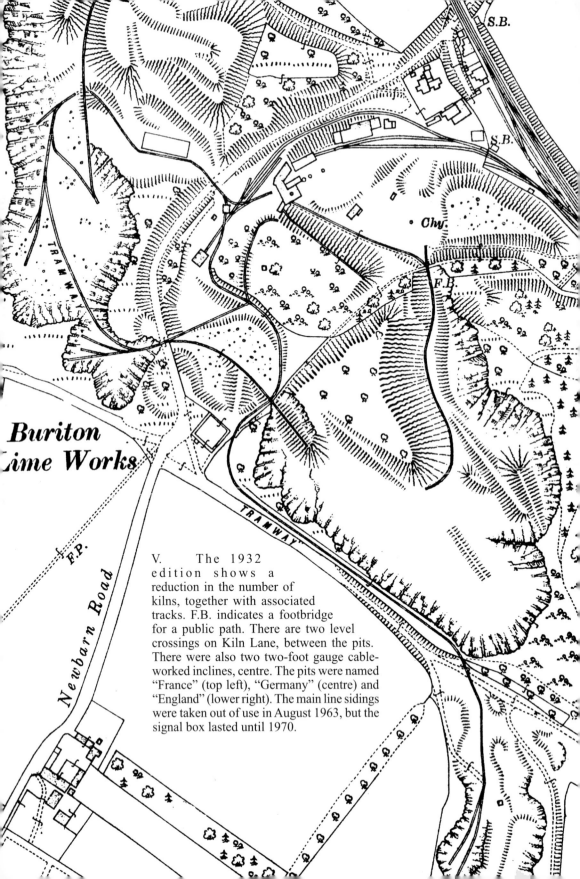

S.B.

S.B.

Chy.

F.B.

TRAMWAY

Buriton
Lime Works

F.P.

Newbarn Road

TRAMWAY

V.   The 1932
edition shows a
reduction in the number of
kilns, together with associated
tracks. F.B. indicates a footbridge
for a public path. There are two level
crossings on Kiln Lane, between the pits.
There were also two two-foot gauge cable-
worked inclines, centre. The pits were named
"France" (top left), "Germany" (centre) and
"England" (lower right). The main line sidings
were taken out of use in August 1963, but the
signal box lasted until 1970.

7.　　　These are the kilns in Germany Pit. The name was probably due to the fact that Hoffman kilns were situated there. The Forder family sold the business to APCM in 1924 and horse traction soon ended. The narrow gauge rails terminate above the seated man's head. (J.Hay coll.)

8.　　　Two Motor Rail Simplex 40hp petrol-engined locomotives were purchased in 1924-25. Both were built for the War Department and had to be regauged from two-foot to three. (J.Hay coll.)

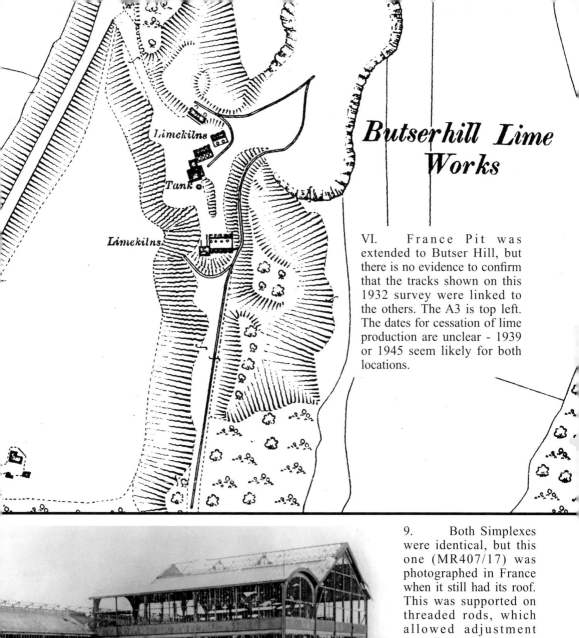

Butserhill Lime Works

VI. France Pit was extended to Butser Hill, but there is no evidence to confirm that the tracks shown on this 1932 survey were linked to the others. The A3 is top left. The dates for cessation of lime production are unclear - 1939 or 1945 seem likely for both locations.

Map labels: Limekilns, Tank, Limekilns

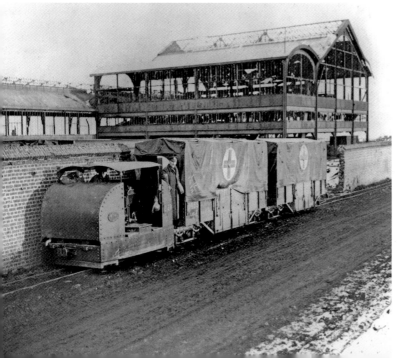

9. Both Simplexes were identical, but this one (MR407/17) was photographed in France when it still had its roof. This was supported on threaded rods, which allowed adjustment according to weather and battle conditions. (J.Hay coll.)

10.   Hunslet no. 4395 was recorded at North Station Pits on 27th June 1964 with a train of empties, when in the ownership of the Twickenham Gravel Company. The wagon frames have been fitted with stays, to prevent them falling over when being emptied. (C.G.Down)

11.   Seen on the same day, but out of use, was Hunslet no. 4396 of 1952. The skip on the right has had tip limit stops fitted for the reason just stated. (C.G.Down)

12. A 1967 record features Hunslet no. 4394 and the mobile loading hopper. This eliminated the problem of wagons being knocked over by the bucket of the drag-line excavator. (P.Nicholson)

13. The conveyor belts in the background of this panorama from March 1970 had taken over from rail transport. Nos 4396, 4395 and 4394 await their fate. (P.Nicholson)

14.	No. 4396 is being loaded for transporting to Brockham; later it went to Greece. Nos 94 and 95 went to the Groudle Glen Railway on the Isle of Man, its gauge also being two-foot. The date is 13th June 1970. (P.Nicholson)

HYTHE PIER RAILWAY

15.   There have been records of a ferry service at Hythe for over 400 years, this having been provided by individuals with sailing wherries until 1830, when a steam vessel was introduced. It made six crossings each weekday, but it did not last long. Plans for a pier were made in 1870, but this did not open until 1st January 1881. The pier is seen in that decade with the ferry *Frederica* alongside. (Postcard)

16.   Rails were laid on the pier in 1909 and porters pushed wagons carrying luggage and merchandise of all types. Hythe did not have a railway station until 1925, when the Southern Railway opened its Fawley branch. Thus most goods came by ferry until that time. (Postcard)

17.   The pier railway was electrically operated from July 1922 and passengers were carried thereafter. A generator provided current at 200 volts initially. One of the three locomotives is seen on 12th April 1952. (J.H.Meredith)

18.   The company had been formed in 1880 as the "Hythe Pier and Hythe and Southampton Ferry Company", and its shares were gradually acquired by the General Estates Company. The linkspan to the pontoon is visible in this view from September 1952. (J.H.Meredith)

19.   The track was laid to two-foot gauge and one siding was provided at the shore end. The photo is from 1955 and includes the workshops, together with a mobile tank which took diesel oil to the ferries until about 1974. (R.Holmes)

20.　　The workshops have to undertake jobs of all types. This 1968 picture shows the rebuilding of one of the Brush locomotives in progress. They had been built to be battery powered for use in an ammunition factory in World War I. (P.Nicholson)

21.　　The shore-end terminus was photographed in October 1989. Services had steadily improved (except in wartime) and, from 1st April 1947, the interval was 30 minutes during weekdays and one hour on Sundays. Trains left three minutes before ferry departure time. (J.H.Meredith)

22.　　This 1989 view features the other teminus together with a luggage wagon and roof improvements. Motor boats became popular between the wars and the last steam ferry was thus converted in 1946. More transport history was made in 1950 when flying boat operation from the neighbouring premises came to an end. (J.H.Meredith)

23.   A 1998 record includes the system's second point and evidence of pier maintenance, loco servicing and staff transport. A decline in revenue took place in 1950 owing to the end of petrol rationing and an increase in private motoring. (T.Wright)

24.   A view at low tide in 1999 emphasises the need for a long pier over the gently sloping foreshore. The superstructure of the ferry (left) and the train were painted white at that time; the train was returned to dark green in 2004. (White Horse Ferries)

25.   A panorama from 22nd May 2003 includes the second fuel oil tanker in the unelectrified siding. Note the long gap in the conductor rail, the voltage of which had for long been increased to 240. (T.Wright)

Hythe's other station is illustrated in our *Southampton to Bournemouth* **album.**

26. The standard formation was recorded on the same day, the leading coach bearing the letters HPR. The ferries were fitted with radar in November 1976, which brought to an end the erratic suspension of service due to fog. (T.Wright)

27. This damage was done by a drunken captain of a dredger on 1st November 2003; the pier remained closed until 6th January 2004. It resulted in a belated change in the law. The track runs into the sea on the left. (White Horse Ferries)

INNS & CO. LTD.
FARNBOROUGH

28.   This gravel pit was partly in Surrey and thus one of its locomotives appears in *Surrey Narrow Gauge* (picture 20). This is Motor Rail no. 4720 and it was pictured on 27th June 1964. Operation had ceased by 1967. (C.G.Down)

PORTSMOUTH SEWER - NUTTALL

29.   As part of Southern Water's £100M investment to provide a modern wastewater treatment system for Portsmouth and Havant, Nuttall was awarded the contract for the design and construction of an 8km long, 2.85m internal diameter transfer tunnel. The tunnel links the wastewater treatment works at Budds Farm, Havant with the Eastney Pumping Station, Portsmouth and was constructed in two 4km lengths from a central site located at Kendall's Wharf. Sewage is pumped in pipeline through the tunnel for treatment at Budds Farm and the cleaned effluent flows by gravity back through the tunnel to Eastney where it is pumped out to sea through the existing 5.7km long outfall. (E.Nuttall)

30.   The work was undertaken in 1998-2001 using two tunnel boring machines and a Clayton electric locomotive of 2ft 6ins gauge. This is seen with a complete set of lining segments. It was also used for the conveyance of grout for filling the voids behind the segment rings. (E.Nuttall)

ROOKLEY BRICKWORKS

31.　　　Situated about three miles south of Newport, the works had a two-foot gauge system of about ¼ mile in length. After closure it was acquired by the Island Narrow Gauge Railway Group and the firm's Ruston & Hornsby diesel was used to aid lifting the Jubilee track. The operation was photographed in June 1972, prior to the equipment being moved to the new Albany Steam and Industrial Museum, see picture 70. (G.Stevens)

ROWLANDS CASTLE BRICKWORKS

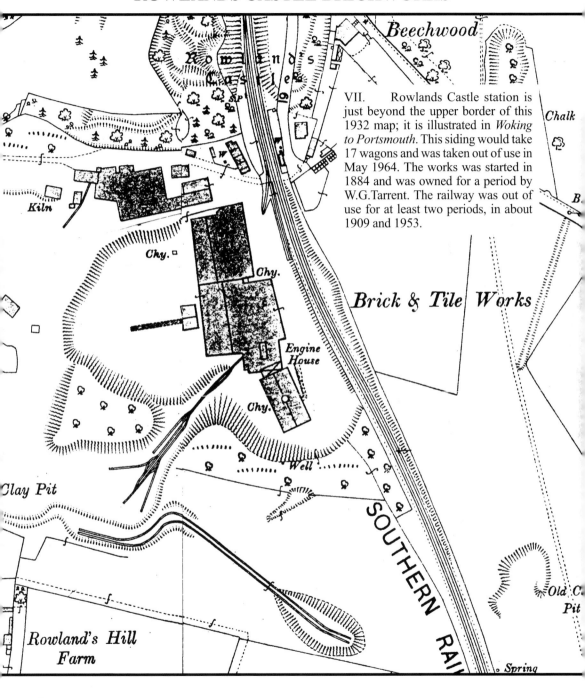

VII.   Rowlands Castle station is just beyond the upper border of this 1932 map; it is illustrated in *Woking to Portsmouth*. This siding would take 17 wagons and was taken out of use in May 1964. The works was started in 1884 and was owned for a period by W. G. Tarrent. The railway was out of use for at least two periods, in about 1909 and 1953.

32.　　　Three photographs from 26th July 1964 follow. The owner was then the Associated Brick & Tile Company. A face shovel was used for loading the tipper wagons. (C.G.Down)

33.　　　Lines from two clay workings converged at this point. The slats on the duckboards gave a good grip for the boots of the labourers. (C.G.Down)

34.　　　This is the lower end of the incline to the works. Empty wagons have been lowered by rope into the siding on the right. Two-foot gauge track was employed. (C.G.Down)

35.   A panorama from above the tunnel mouth on 19th February 1985 has Southampton Central station in the background. There is a two-foot gauge track each side of the main lines; only one of these was in use during tunnel repairs. The structure had been partly intended for a canal and was started in about 1803. The brick lining was being replaced after about 140 years of railway use. (V.Mitchell)

36.   The first step was to reconstruct the invert with reinforced concrete and to lay on its edges two channels on which this special gantry could run. The brickwork was removed from above. This was used as a working platform and was designed to take the full force of a roof fall. One narrow gauge track is in the foreground. (E.Nuttall)

37.   The line on the south side was used for transporting concrete, grouting and lining segments, while the one on the other side conveyed mainly brick rubble and segments. The work took almost two years. The site had once been close to the beach, as explained in our *Southampton to Bournemouth* album. (V.Mitchell)

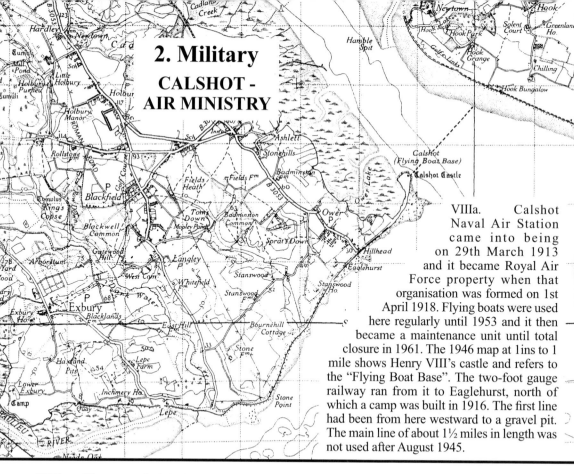

2. Military
CALSHOT - AIR MINISTRY

VIIIa. Calshot Naval Air Station came into being on 29th March 1913 and it became Royal Air Force property when that organisation was formed on 1st April 1918. Flying boats were used here regularly until 1953 and it then became a maintenance unit until total closure in 1961. The 1946 map at 1ins to 1 mile shows Henry VIII's castle and refers to the "Flying Boat Base". The two-foot gauge railway ran from it to Eaglehurst, north of which a camp was built in 1916. The first line had been from here westward to a gravel pit. The main line of about 1½ miles in length was not used after August 1945.

VIIIb.   The east end of the line was almost entirely surrounded by sea. (A.Neale coll.)

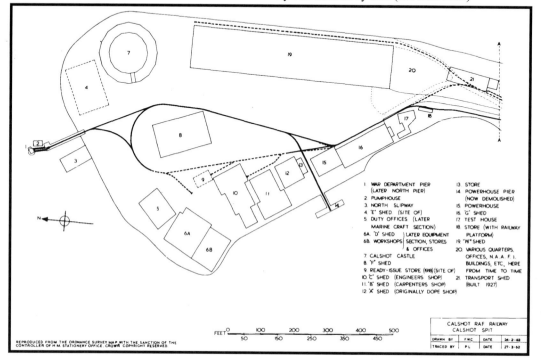

1 WAR DEPARTMENT PIER (LATER NORTH PIER)
2 PUMPHOUSE
3 NORTH SLIPWAY
4 'E' SHED (SITE OF)
5 DUTY OFFICES (LATER MARINE CRAFT SECTION)
6A 'D' SHED } LATER EQUIPMENT
6B WORKSHOPS } SECTION, STORES & OFFICES
7 CALSHOT CASTLE
8 'F' SHED
9 READY-ISSUE STORE (RAB) (SITE OF)
10 'C' SHED (ENGINEERS SHOP)
11 'B' SHED (CARPENTERS SHOP)
12 'A' SHED (ORIGINALLY DOPE SHOP)
13 STORE
14 POWERHOUSE PIER (NOW DEMOLISHED)
15 POWERHOUSE
16 'G' SHED
17 TEST HOUSE
18 STORE (WITH RAILWAY PLATFORM)
19 'H' SHED
20 VARIOUS QUARTERS, OFFICES, N.A.A.F.I. BUILDINGS, ETC, HERE FROM TIME TO TIME
21 TRANSPORT SHED (BUILT 1927)

N

FEET 0 100 200 300 400 500
50 150 250 350 450

CALSHOT RAF RAILWAY CALSHOT SPIT			
DRAWN BY	FWC	DATE	24·2·62
TRACED BY	PL	DATE	27·3·62

REPRODUCED FROM THE ORDNANCE SURVEY MAP WITH THE SANCTION OF THE CONTROLLER OF H.M. STATIONERY OFFICE. CROWN COPYRIGHT RESERVED

38. Barclay 0-4-0WTs of this type were the main source of power on the line after 1921. Two petrol-engined Baguleys were in service in 1918-20. This is the guard room and gate on Spit Road. Usually only one of the two Barclays was in steam at a time. (Postcard)

39. Early locomotive records are incomplete, but a Kerr Stuart "Wren" class 0-4-0T was in use in 1920. This is probably no. 4019. (P.Q.Treloar coll.)

VIIIc. The west of the route was close to the village of Ower. (A.Neale coll.)

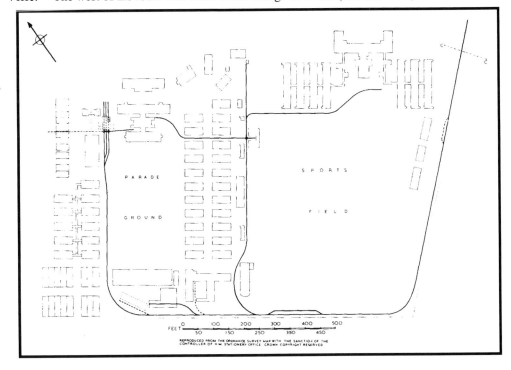

PARADE GROUND

SPORTS FIELD

FEET 0   100   200   300   400   500
      50   150   250   350   450

REPRODUCED FROM THE ORDNANCE SURVEY MAP WITH THE SANCTION OF THE CONTROLLER OF H M STATIONERY OFFICE CROWN COPYRIGHT RESERVED

40. The main hangar is now occupied by the Calshot Activity Centre and forms the backdrop for this view of another Barclay product. The track layout changed over the years at both ends of the route. (J.K.Williams coll.)

41. The line crossed the public road near the officers mess near which the gradient was 1 in 12. The road became RAF property in about 1939. There was a three-road engine shed at Eaglehurst and locomotives always faced inland, owing to the incline. (Postcard)

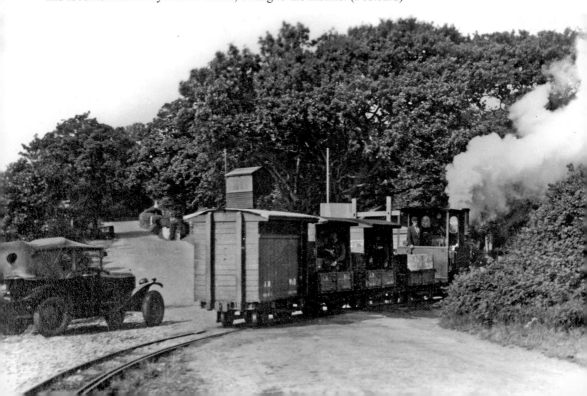

42.   *Douglas* made a one-day return visit to Calshot on 14th March 1996, during its journey from temporary exhibition at the RAF Museum at Hendon to the Talyllyn Railway. Lower right is a cut-out of Dolgoch Viaduct. The line is fully illustrated in *Talyllyn - 50 Years of Change*. AM. W&B is Air Ministry Works & Buildings. (M.Turvey)

DEAN HILL
DEFENCE MUNITIONS DEPOT

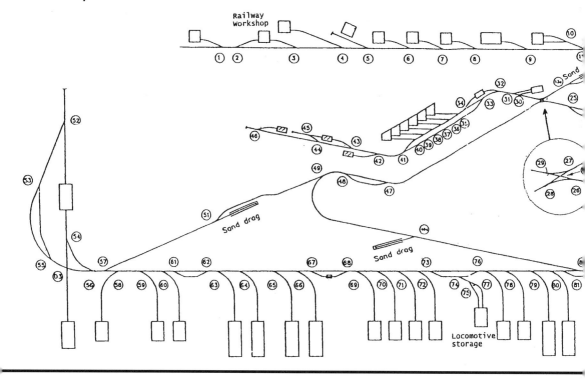

43.   The depot was initially provided with 50hp diesel Hunslet 0-4-0s, fitted with special flameproof exhaust conditioning. This is no. 2254 of 1940 and it was photographed in 1968. (P.Nicholson)

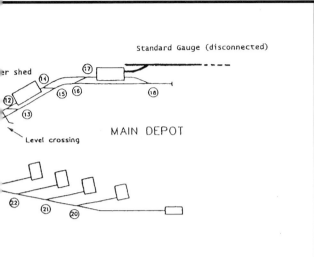

Standard Gauge (disconnected)

er shed

⑭
⑫ ⑮ ⑯ ⑰ ⑱
⑬

Level crossing

MAIN DEPOT

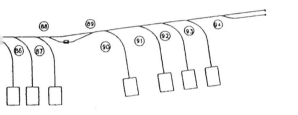

㉒ ㉑ ⑳

IX.   The site was developed in 1942 as a Royal Naval Armaments Depot intended to serve the Portsmouth and Gosport area. Top right is the standard gauge siding which was in use until 1993. The line of stores along the bottom of the diagram represents subterranean caverns or magazines.

⑧⑧ ⑧⑨ ㉔
⑧⑥ ⑧⑦ ⑨⓪ ⑨① ⑨② ⑨③

44.   The same locomotive is seen on the top level with a van train containing small munitions. The curve leads to one of the underground stores. One of these engines (no. 2251) was acquired by the Welshpool & Llanfair Railway in 1972. (P.Nicholson)

45.　　A train carrying 1000lb bombs on pallets is seen at the same location. It is hauled by one of the second generation of diesels, which were provided by Hunslets during the mid-1960s. (P.Nicholson)

→

46.　　This and the following photographs were taken on 17th September 2003 after removal of the bombs from the site and just prior to the closure of the depot. We start our tour at the top right corner of the diagram with a look at the engine shed, which had two 2ft 6ins gauge tracks still in use. On the right is a remnant of the standard gauge siding. The remainder had been lifted in 1996. (V.Mitchell)

→

47.　　Inside the shed were no. 294, Hunslet 6652 of 1965, and no. 884 Baguley-Drewry 3752 of 1980, on the left. The speed limit was 10mph and above that a siren sounded. (V.Mitchell)

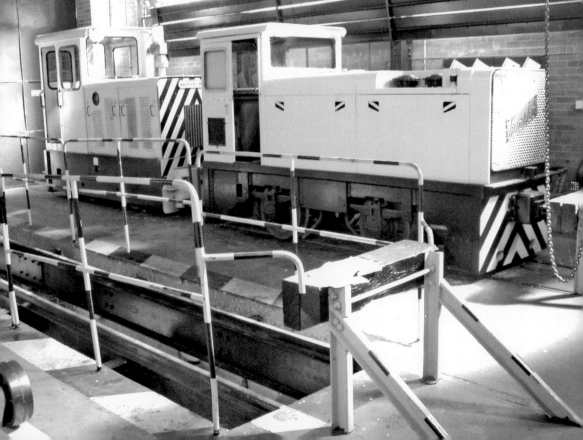

48.　　A photo taken outside the shed includes the eastern end of the line and a four-wheeled coach attached to Baguley-Drewry no. 887 ready for the tour. (V.Mitchell)

49.　　A climb up the first incline brought the train to a complex of points numbered 26 to 29. On the right is a convex mirror for added safety at the junction. (V.Mitchell)

50.	An eastward view at the junction shows the chalk ridge of the downs, below which a bank hides the entrances to the 24 buried storage chambers. (V.Mitchell)

51.	West of the crossing, the main line continues to climb on the right. On the left are workshops into which bombs were taken for regular examination and servicing. Six sidings diverge from the loop. (V.Mitchell)

52.   To find this location on the diagram, look for points 44 and 45. There was a total of 94 points in the five miles of track which was electrically bonded to reduce the risk of lightning strikes causing problems. (V.Mitchell)

53.   We are near point 55, on the left of the diagram and are looking at the transfer shed used by lorries. Closure of the main line siding resulted in explosives travelling by road to and from the site. (V.Mitchell)

54.   On the right is an additional guard house provided near the entrance to the store used for nuclear material. On the left is the tour coach (no. 555), which was normally used for staff transport. (V.Mitchell)

→

55.   The tour concluded with a visit to one of the highly secure stores. Welsh miners had been brought here in 1939 to begin the massive excavation task. It would have made a change for them to finish work white, instead of black. (D.G.Salter)

56.   The doors were opened and the party crept into the air-conditioned chamber. There was a proliferation of fire fighting equipment, inside and out. Phosphoro-bronze rails were used inside the magazines to eliminate spark risk. (V.Mitchell)

→

57.   The floor was built level with the tops of the wagons and an overhead travelling crane was provided in many of the stores. There were nine locomotives (not all usable), 174 flat wagons, nine with bogies, ten vans and four fork lift transporters, plus ramp wagons. From 1st April 1999, the site was in the charge of the Defence Logistics Organisation and was designated an SSSI. (V.Mitchell)

HASLAR HOSPITAL

58.   The camera is on the dual gauge track from the jetty and the 18ins gauge line curves left towards the waterfront. (J.B.Horne coll.)

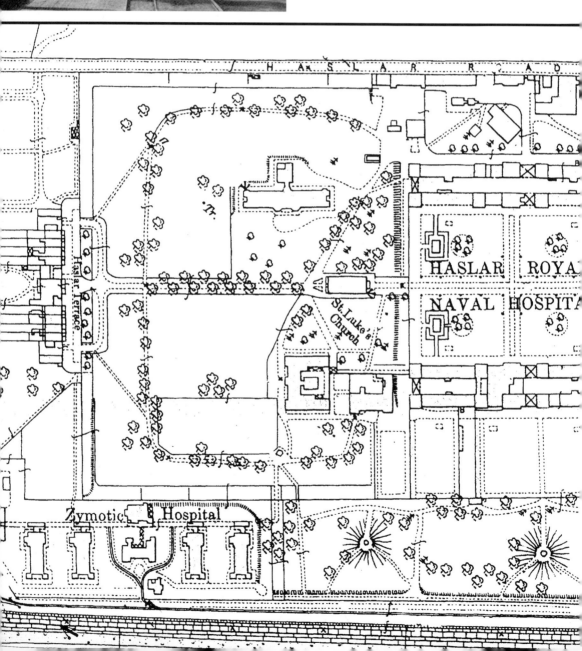

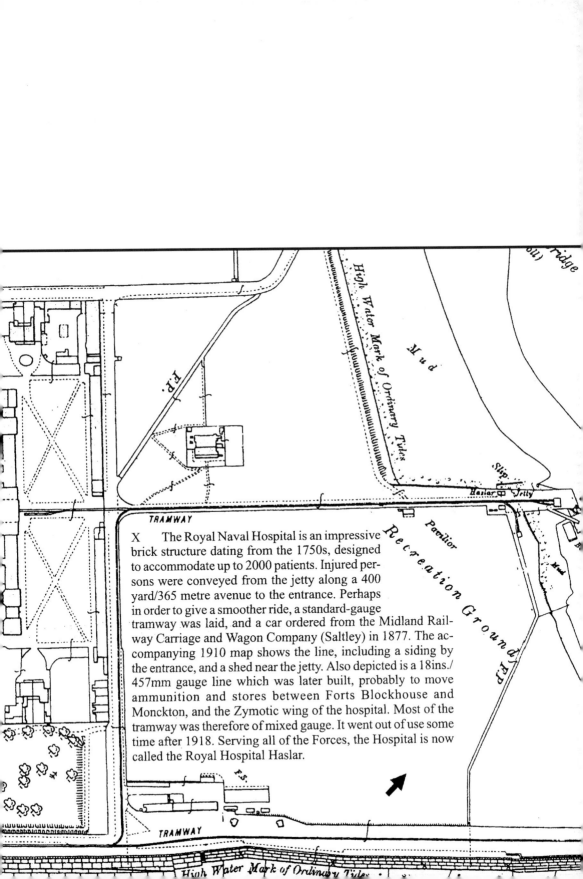

TRAMWAY

X   The Royal Naval Hospital is an impressive brick structure dating from the 1750s, designed to accommodate up to 2000 patients. Injured persons were conveyed from the jetty along a 400 yard/365 metre avenue to the entrance. Perhaps in order to give a smoother ride, a standard-gauge tramway was laid, and a car ordered from the Midland Railway Carriage and Wagon Company (Saltley) in 1877. The accompanying 1910 map shows the line, including a siding by the entrance, and a shed near the jetty. Also depicted is a 18ins./457mm gauge line which was later built, probably to move ammunition and stores between Forts Blockhouse and Monckton, and the Zymotic wing of the hospital. Most of the tramway was therefore of mixed gauge. It went out of use some time after 1918. Serving all of the Forces, the Hospital is now called the Royal Hospital Haslar.

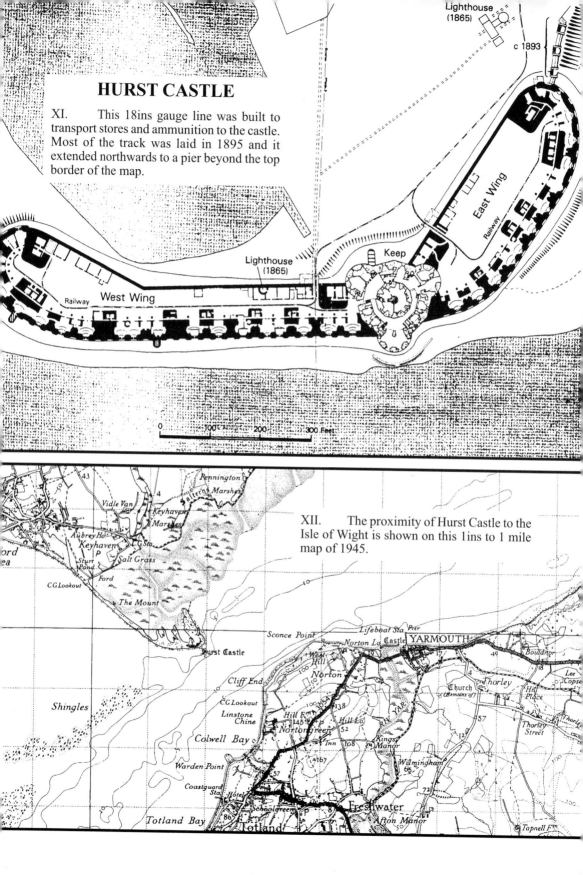

HURST CASTLE

XI.   This 18ins gauge line was built to transport stores and ammunition to the castle. Most of the track was laid in 1895 and it extended northwards to a pier beyond the top border of the map.

Lighthouse (1865)

c 1893

East Wing
Railway

Lighthouse (1865)

Keep

Railway

West Wing

0   100   200   300 Feet

XII.   The proximity of Hurst Castle to the Isle of Wight is shown on this 1ins to 1 mile map of 1945.

Pennington Marshes

Vidle Van

Keyhaven Marshes

Aubrey Ho.
Keyhaven
Salt Grass
Sturt Pond
Ford
C.G.Lookout
The Mount

Hurst Castle

Shingles

Sconce Point
Lifeboat Sta. Pier
Norton Lo. Castle
YARMOUTH
Bouldnor

Cliff End
West Hill
Norton
Church (Remains of)
Thorley
Hill Place
Lee Copse

C.G.Lookout
Linstone Chine
Hill Ft.
Hill Lo.
Nortongreen
Kings Manor
Thorley Street

Colwell Bay
Inn
Wilmingham

Warden Point

Coastguard Sta.
Hotel
Afton Manor
Tapnell Fm.

Totland Bay
Schoolgreen
Totland
Freshwater

59.　　　The line from the jetty is in the foreground and the one on the left leads to the East Wing. The West Wing is in the background. All the photos are from April 2004. (R.Rundle)

60.　　　This is a northward view inside the gate of the East Wing. Locomotives were never used; a donkey was the normal power. (R.Rundle)

61.　　　Looking in the other direction, we see the same points and part of the structure of East Wing. (R.Rundle)

62.　　The West Wing gate is seen from outside, the track passing over a draw bridge between the chains. (R.Rundle)

63.   A westward view inside the West Wing gates includes the 1865 lighthouse (right) which was accessed through a doorway on the outside of the fortification. The lighthouse on the left was built in 1911; the first had been erected in 1786. (R.Rundle)

64.	Some of the guns from the 1870s remained in working order until 1918. The West Wing gates are on the left of this view in the opposite direction from the last one. (R.Rundle)

65.	The main purpose of the railway is revealed in this photograph. The battery was modernised in the 1930s and manned during World War II. It ceased to be operational in 1956 and is now cared for by English Heritage. (R.Rundle)

WOOLMER INSTRUCTIONAL MILITARY RAILWAY

66.　　This was the title used from 1908 until 1935, when the standard gauge Longmoor Military Railway came into being. Work began in 1903, when two parallel 18ins gauge tracks were laid to convey huts from Bordon using horse power and cables from ploughing engines. Three locomotives of this gauge arrived from Chatham Dockyard in 1905 to assist with the construction work. This is *Flamingo*, a Fowler 0-4-2T completed in 1885. (Unknown)

67.　　Track ballast for the standard gauge line and building materials for the camp were conveyed in large quantities. Recorded on Weavers Down is *Mars*, a Vulcan Foundry 0-4-2T of 1886. The third engine was *Venus*, a sister of *Mars*. They had been supplied new to Woolwich Arsenal. (Unknown)

68.   Previously numbered 3239, this two-foot gauge 4-6-0T had been built by the Hunslet Engine Company in 1919 and was used on the Stokes Bay Military Railway, near Gosport. It did not run at Longmoor, but was there for instructional purposes only. It was photographed in 1961. (T.Wright)

69.   On site for the same reason in 1948 were two German Wehrmacht 0-6-0 diesels on 75cm track. They were thought to be in use on rocket launch sites earlier and remained on the Weavers Down Light Railway until 1957. The LMR closed on 31st October 1969 and is fully illustrated in our *Branch Lines to Longmoor*. (S.W.Baker)

3. Pleasure

ALBANY STEAM MUSEUM
FOREST ROAD LIGHT RAILWAY

⟶

70.   The museum was established on a site about one mile northwest of Newport and some of the equipment from Rookley Brickworks (see picture 31) was moved there to form the Forest Road Light Railway. A Simplex is seen, along with a modified tipper wagon. (G.Stevens)

71.   Steam traction was provided by *Peter Pan*, a Kerr Stuart product of 1922. Planning consent was refused, but given later, upon appeal. By that time the museum closure was planned and the track was lifted. The locomotive eventually went to the Leighton Buzzard Railway, via the Dowty Preservation Society at Ashchurch, Gloucestershire. (G.Stevens)

⟶

72.   A May 1973 photograph features the ex-Rookley Brickworks Ruston & Hornsby 16/20 diesel of 1937. It cost £450 when new and could haul 70 tons on the level. (G.Stevens)

BURSLEDON BRICKWORKS

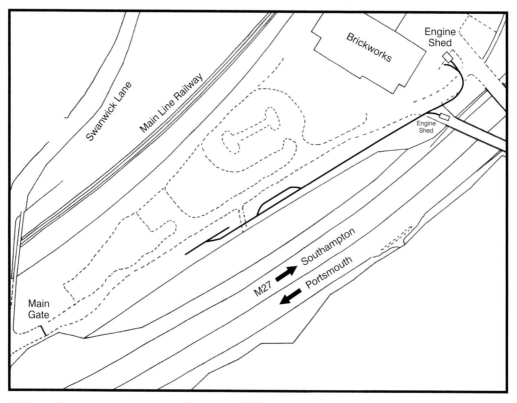

XIII.   The brickworks was established in 1897, and it had its own railway system to the clay pits in its early years. Subsequently, overhead conveyors were used until the works closed in 1974. A trust was formed to conserve the premises and to establish demonstrations of brickmaking and other crafts. (R.Carpenter)

73.   Two locomotives arrived at the end of 1996 and laying of Jubilee track began early in 1997. Motor Rail Simplex no. 8694 *Beccy* was photographed on 16th May 1999. (P.Nicholson)

74. Seen on the same day (from left to right) are Hunslet no. 3653 ex-Thakenham Tiles, Ransomes & Rapier no. 80 of 1937 and Motor Rail no. 5226. The first two were visitors from Amberley Working Museum. (P.Nicholson)

75. The Hampshire Narrow Gauge Railway Society brought much equipment to the site including *Wendy*, a Bagnall 0-4-0 ST built in 1919. This arrived from Kew Bridge Steam Museum shortly before being photographed on 20th July 2003. (P.G.Barnes)

76. *Wendy* was demonstrating a typical brickworks train on the light track. She had been fully restored in 1979. Heavier rail was used on the extensions. (P.G.Barnes)

DURLEY LIGHT RAILWAY

77.   The Hampshire Narrow Gauge Railway Society's collection began at Stoke Park sand pit, Bishopstoke, about one mile east of Eastleigh, in 1962. Members are working on AGWI PET which was donated by ESSO. In the background is the original name of the Society. (HNGRS coll.)

78. The HNGRS moved to Durley, approximately four miles east of Eastleigh, in 1968 and set about erecting accommodation and creating a circular demonstration track. This is the first of four photographs from 8th April 1972. (P.Nicholson)

79. The site was far from level and much labour was necessary to create embankments. To achieve this, a tipper wagon body and frame was mounted on another frame to allow end tipping. (P.Nicholson)

80.　　Two surveying poles were apt supports for the tape cut upon the opening of the circuit. *Cloister* waits to pass over the culvert, which required substantial wing walls for the bridging. (P.Nicholson)

81.　　*Cloister* was built by the Hunslet Engine Company in 1891 and worked for most of its life in the Dinorwic Slate Quarry. The coach was built for the Ramsgate Tunnel Railway, which is featured in our *Kent Narrow Gauge*. Both items belonged to the HNGRS, which removed all its stock from the site in 1992, these two items eventually going to the Kew Bridge Steam Museum - see *Surrey Narrow Gauge*. (P.Nicholson)

82.   *Wendy* went to Kew Bridge in 1993. It is seen on 10th July 1982, lettered DLR No. 1. It had been built by Bagnall in 1919 and had also served the Welsh slate industry. *Wendy* moved from Kew to the Bursledon Brickworks in the Summer of 2003. (M.Turvey)

83.   Two photos from the same open day follow. This includes the body of Mr. Drummond's inspection saloon which had been attached to one of his LSWR locomotives. This remnant of "The Bug" was removed later for care by the Drummond Society. (M.Turvey)

84.   Demonstrating its pulling power that day was a 1936 Orenstein & Koppel two-cylinder diesel. Some of the HNGRS equipment was transferred to the East Hayling Light Railway in 1992. This loco had hauled ball clay at Norden in Dorset for many years and remained at Durley. (M.Turvey)

85.   The site owners operated their own stock after 1992 and continued to hold occasional open days. DLR No. 2 is seen on 18th July 1996. This 0-4-2T was new in 1936 from the Hunslet Engine Company to the British Aluminium Corporation at Fort William and had to be regauged from 3ft. They also have a 1918 Feldbahn 0-8-0T from Hanomag, which had worked in France. (D.Trevor Rowe)

EAST HAYLING LIGHT RAILWAY

86.   The railway has operated on two sites on Hayling Island, the first being at Mill Rythe Holiday Village. The first two pictures are at that location and date from 28th June 2000. Work had started here in 1988 with less than 10 volunteers. (T.Mercer)

XIV.   Diagram of the railway at Mill Rythe Holiday Village.

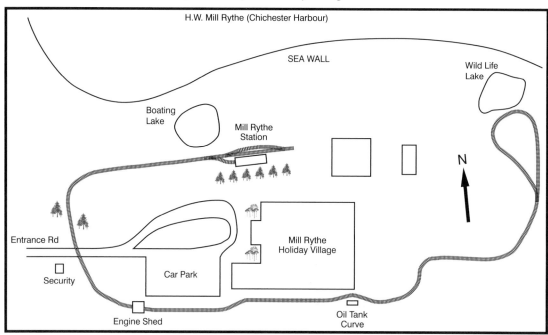

87.   The steam outline body of 0-4-0 *Jack* conceals a 2.8 litre diesel engine with hydraulic transmission. Until 1990, intending passengers had to purchase a day ticket to enter the site, which limited numbers to 5000 or so. (T.Mercer)

88.   The last train ran on 30th September 2001 and this photograph was taken a week later as dismantling began. On the left is *Ace*, which was to be out of loading gauge for the new line, but was subjected to surgery later. It was built in 1937 by Motor Rail and fitted with a Lister engine in 1976. (T.Mercer)

89.   Work on the new seafront line was well advanced when this photo was taken on 11th April 2002. The section on the left would serve as the terminus/carriage shed and that on the right would be the workshop. (T.Mercer)

90.   Free transport was provided by the lorry owner for the entire move. By the time that this picture was taken in May 2002, there were over 100 other volunteers on this imaginative project. We see *Ace* again, soon to be renamed *Alan B*. The other engine is *Alistair*, a 1941 Ruston & Hornsby 0-4-0 diesel ex-Gartell Light Railway. (T.Mercer)

91.   Much labour went into laying the track, which has staggered joints. Almost 2000 concrete sleepers were cast individually by members. This idea was put forward in 1951 for the Festiniog Railway, but not pursued. (P.Nicholson)

92.   This is the prospective passenger's perspective prior to a journey taken to the end of the line at Eastoke on 7th December 2003. *Jack* is running round its train and is standing near the redundant mobile booking office. The station is located near the Funland Amusement Park. (V.Mitchell)

93.   Moments later it is backing onto its train, which is standing under the overall roof, a feature of great benefit to winter travellers. The trackwork can be appreciated in this westward view of Beachlands station. (V.Mitchell)

94.	The extent of the roof is evident as *Jack* awaits the green flag. The brakes and whistle are air operated. The balcony coach no. 6 *Joanna* is leading. (V.Mitchell)

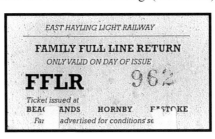

EAST HAYLING LIGHT RAILWAY

FAMILY FULL LINE RETURN

ONLY VALID ON DAY OF ISSUE

FFLR	962

Ticket issued at
BEAC ANDS	HORNBY	F STOKE
Far   advertised for conditions se

95.   The guard is waiting for the photographer to record Hornby Halt as the shadows lengthen. Trains on Wednesdays, Saturdays and Sundays are of particular value to local residents throughout the Winter. (V.Mitchell)

96.   *Jack* reaches the terminus at Eastoke. The mobile booking office was named *Colin M* and had stood on the right, but problems arose when tickets were sold for trains that were already full. The van was therefore sold to the Old Kiln Railway and the guard issued tickets. (V.Mitchell)

97. Having run round, *Jack* is ready to return to Beachlands with the last train of the day. More than 20,000 passengers had been carried in the first season. (V.Mitchell)

98. The full extent of the loop is now seen. A bogie coach would be ready for the next Summer season on this one-mile long line operated to high standards by truly dedicated enthusiasts. The line was renamed Hayling Seaside Railway in April 2004, as plans were made for a 1½ mile extension westward to the ferry to Portsmouth. (V.Mitchell)

EXBURY GARDENS RAILWAY

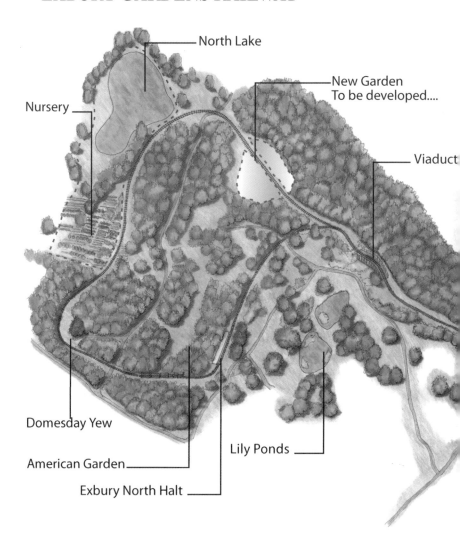

XV.   The Rothschild family has been involved in financing and constructing railways on an international scale since the 1830s. It is no surprise that a descendant of these pioneers, Leopold de Rothschild, should be inspired to create a small railway to high and traditional standards in the magnificent gardens laid out by his father between the wars. The diagram indicates the joys of both and the extent of the 1¼ mile-long journey on 12¼ ins gauge track. The line opened on 3rd August 2001 and around 10,000 people travelled by the end of November. The figures for 2002 were 48,000 and 2003 totalled 50,300.

99.   Work began in September 2000 and the erection of the steelwork for the station superstructure was soon underway. In the foreground is the base for the ticket office. (Exbury Gardens)

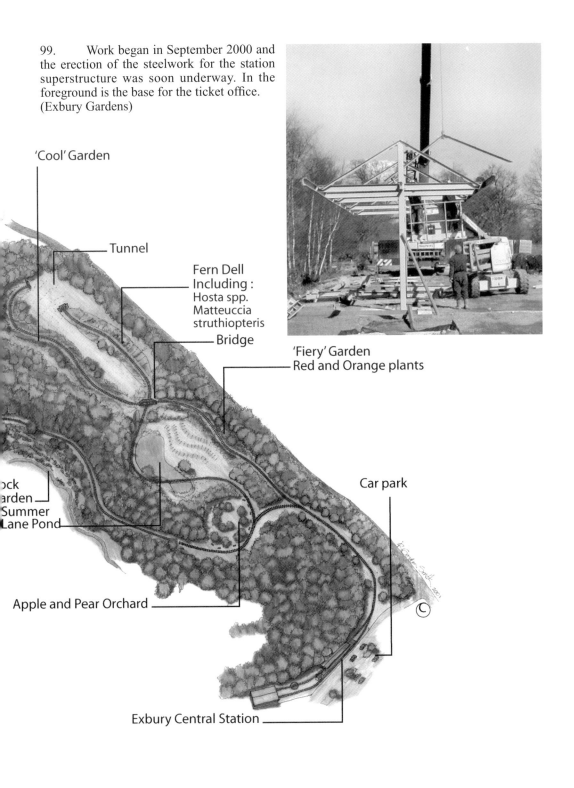

'Cool' Garden

Tunnel

Fern Dell
Including :
Hosta spp.
Matteuccia
struthiopteris

Bridge

'Fiery' Garden
Red and Orange plants

ock
arden
Summer
Lane Pond

Car park

Apple and Pear Orchard

Exbury Central Station

100.　　Almost 200 people were engaged for differing periods on the civil engineering and track laying, some of which is on gradients of 1 in 50. More than 60,000 new plants and trees were included in the scheme. (Exbury Gardens)

101.   Two steam locomotives were built for the line by the Exmoor Steam Railway, works numbers 315 and 316, and both were 0-6-2Ts. *Rosemary* was delivered in July 2001. This and the following three photographs were taken in 2002-03. (Janet Smith)

102.   *Naomi* was from the same drawings and arrived in September 2002. Both engines were named after the owner's sisters. The cab seats two in comfort. (T.Wright)

103.   The 0-4-2T *Denzil* was on loan from the locomotive builder for the 2002 season and is seen on the hand-operated turntable between the station and the locomotive shed. (Janet Smith)

EXBURY GARDENS RAILWAY

EXPRESS TICKET
between
XBURY CENTRAL
and
EXBURY NORTH

02295

104.   A four-ton diesel was being built at Bratton Fleming in Devon and was to be named *Eddy* after the brother in the family. This unit was on loan from Exmoor Steam Railway. (T.Wright)

105.   We now have five photographs taken on 14th December 2003 when seasonal decorations had been added. *Naomi* stands with the maximum load of 64 passengers at the canopy which was modelled on Aviemore. (V.Mitchell)

106.   *Rosemary* was also in steam and stands ahead of the signals. There is one more signal, this being on the approach to the station. Others were planned. (V.Mitchell)

107.   A panorama of Exbury Central includes locomotives being lit up in the early morning outside a classical three-road engine shed that must be the envy of many locomen. Stone keystones and capitals add style and charm. (V.Mitchell)

108.   "Exbury North - Alight for the American Garden" states the nameboard as *Rosemary* calls on her scenic journey. There are colourful pleasures to be had in most seasons. (V.Mitchell)

109. The viaduct is one of the memorable structures on the route. There is also a lattice girder bridge further east, as shown on the map. (V.Mitchell)

→

110. As elsewhere, no expense was spared, even on the tunnel portals. The columns are surmounted by the family symbol, which features five arrows. It is also included in the station canopy brackets. (Exbury Gardens)

→

111. A royal visit was made on 8th May 2004 when Her Majesty Queen Elizabeth II rode on *Rosemary*. The experience was obviously greatly enjoyed. (Exbury Gardens)

MARWELL ZOO RAILWAY

112.   Marwell Zoological Park opened in 1972 and the 15 ins gauge railway came into use on 15th April 1987. The four coaches will each accommodate about 30 people. The photo is from June 1991. (M.Turvey)

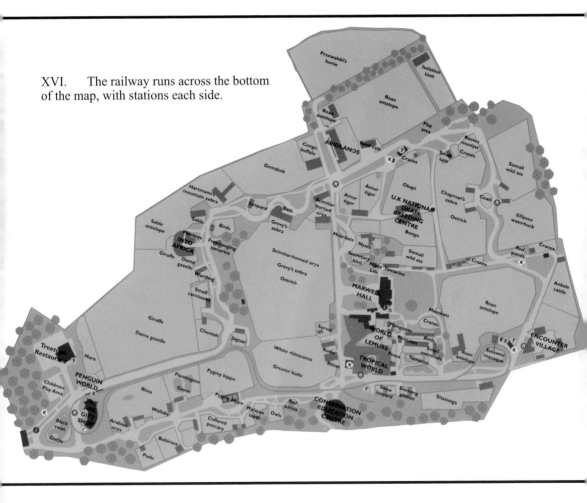

XVI.   The railway runs across the bottom of the map, with stations each side.

113.   The steam outline 2-6-0 *Princess Anne* was built by Severn Lamb with a Perkins diesel engine and named by HRH in 1987. MWR refers to Marwell's Wonderful Railway. (D.Trevor Rowe)

PAULTONS PARK

114.   The park extends for 140 acres and includes beautiful landscaped gardens, together with entertaining rides. The most notable is a 15 ins gauge railway, which was opened in 1986. Some of the five 16-seater coaches are in this view from 18th July 1996. (D.Trevor Rowe)

115.   The Rio Grande Railway locomotive was built by Severn Lamb in 1986 and was fitted with a 4102 Perkins diesel engine. The line carries over 300,000 people annually and is at Ower, near Romsey. (Paultons Park)

XVII.   The railway is lower right on the brochure, but part of its circuit is not included. Train travel is included in the admission charge.

SURREY LIGHT RAILWAY

XVIII.   This private railway was situated in Hampshire at Hook. It had previously been at Hersham, hence its name, and is shown in picture 80 in *Surrey Narrow Gauge*. The diagram is not to scale, but indicates the extent of the trackwork in 1991.

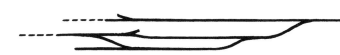

116.   Five photographs were taken during an open day on 18th August 1991. Assorted historic stock is included, and on the right is the triangular form of a new body for a slate slab wagon. Close ups follow of the two diesel locomotives. The low profile one is battery-electric. (I.Oughton)

117.   Ancient items at the other end of the line included a stub point and slate wagons. (P.Nicholson)

→

118. Ruston no. 22 had a 20hp Dorman Long engine and dated from 1944. Other interesting stock is in the background. (I.Oughton)

119. Ruston & Hornsby no. 24 was fitted with a 30hp power unit and was built in 1955 with full weather protection. The life of the line was short and completion of track lifting took place in June 2003, much of the stock going to the Great Bush Railway, seen in pictures 82-88 in *Sussex Narrow Gauge*. (I.Oughton)

→

120. Star of the show in many eyes was a Hunslet 0-4-0ST from Port Dinorwic. It was built in 1922 and carried a cast plate on its boiler showing "No. 1". (P.Nicholson)

YAFFORD MILL

——————→

121.   Construction began in April 1994 and the 2ft 6ins gauge line opened in April 1995. The 450yds of track was extended later. Two Hunslet 0-4-0 diesels of 1940 manufacture were obtained and both had spark arresting exhaust filters. (P.Nicholson)

122.   The coaches were built in 1982 by Alan Keef Ltd and each would accommodate 40 passengers. Air brakes were fitted. There was a run-round loop at each end of the ¾ mile-long line, but latterly it was a P-shaped route. It was about six miles southwest of Newport. (P.Nicholson)

——————→

123.   The other locomotive was similar, but had a shorter exhaust pipe. The wagons were all ex-MoD and were used to carry supplies and materials to other parts of Farm Park. The system closed down and was removed on 11th November 2000, following sale of the premises. Most of the items went to the Sunshine Peat Company in Armagh and the South lost another and unusual narrow gauge line. (P.Nicholson)

Middleton Press

Easebourne Lane, Midhurst, W Sussex. GU29 9AZ Tel: 01730 813169 Fax: 01730 812601
Email: sales@middletonpress.co.uk   www.middletonpress.co.uk

If books are not available from your local transport stockist, order direct post free UK.

BRANCH LINES
Branch Line to Allhallows
Branch Line to Alton
Branch Lines around Ascot
Branch Line to Ashburton
Branch Lines around Bodmin
Branch Line to Bude
Branch Lines around Canterbury
Branch Lines around Chard & Yeovil
Branch Line to Cheddar
Branch Lines around Cromer
Branch Line to the Derwent Valley
Branch Lines to East Grinstead
Branch Lines of East London
Branch Lines to Effingham Junction
Branch Lines to Enfield Town & Palace Gates
Branch Lines to Falmouth, Helston & St. Ives
Branch Line to Fairford
Branch Lines to Felixstowe & Aldeburgh
Branch Lines around Gosport
Branch Line to Hayling
Branch Lines to Henley, Windsor & Marlow
Branch Line to Hawkhurst
Branch Line to Horsham
Branch Lines around Huntingdon
Branch Line to Ilfracombe
Branch Line to Kingsbridge
Branch Line to Kingswear
Branch Line to Lambourn
Branch Lines to Launceston & Princetown
Branch Lines to Longmoor
Branch Line to Looe
Branch Line to Lyme Regis
Branch Line to Lynton
Branch Lines around March
Branch Lines around Midhurst
Branch Line to Minehead
Branch Line to Moretonhampstead
Branch Lines to Newport (IOW)
Branch Line to Newquay
Branch Lines around North Woolwich
Branch Line to Padstow
Branch Lines around Plymouth
Branch Lines to Princes Risborough
Branch Lines to Seaton and Sidmouth
Branch Lines around Sheerness
Branch Line to Shrewsbury
Branch Line to Tenterden
Branch Lines around Tiverton
Branch Lines to Torrington
Branch Lines to Tunbridge Wells
Branch Line to Upwell
Branch Line to Wantage (The Wantage Tramway)
Branch Lines of West London
Branch Lines of West Wiltshire
Branch Lines around Weymouth
Branch Lines around Wimborne
Branch Lines around Wisbech

NARROW GAUGE
Austrian Narrow Gauge
Branch Line to Lynton
Branch Lines around Portmadoc 1923-46
Branch Lines around Porthmadog 1954-94
Branch Line to Southwold
Douglas to Port Erin
Douglas to Peel
Kent Narrow Gauge
Northern France Narrow Gauge
Romneyrail
Sierra Leone Narrow Gauge
Southern France Narrow Gauge
Sussex Narrow Gauge
Surrey Narrow Gauge

Swiss Narrow Gauge
Two-Foot Gauge Survivors
Vivarais Narrow Gauge

SOUTH COAST RAILWAYS
Ashford to Dover
Bournemouth to Weymouth
Brighton to Eastbourne
Brighton to Worthing
Dover to Ramsgate
Eastbourne to Hastings
Hastings to Ashford
Ryde to Ventnor
Southampton to Bournemouth

SOUTHERN MAIN LINES
Basingstoke to Salisbury
Crawley to Littlehampton
Dartford to Sittingbourne
East Croydon to Three Bridges
Epsom to Horsham
Exeter to Barnstaple
Exeter to Tavistock
London Bridge to East Croydon
Tonbridge to Hastings
Salisbury to Yeovil
Sittingbourne to Ramsgate
Swanley to Ashford
Tavistock to Plymouth
Three Bridges to Brighton
Victoria to Bromley South
Victoria to East Croydon
Waterloo to Windsor
Waterloo to Woking
Woking to Portsmouth
Woking to Southampton
Yeovil to Exeter

EASTERN MAIN LINES
Barking to Southend
Ely to Kings Lynn
Ely to Norwich
Fenchurch Street to Barking
Hitchin to Peterborough
Ilford to Shenfield
Ipswich to Saxmundham
Liverpool Street to Ilford
Saxmundham to Yarmouth
Tilbury Loop

WESTERN MAIN LINES
Banbury to Birmingham
Bristol to Taunton
Didcot to Banbury
Didcot to Swindon
Ealing to Slough
Exeter to Newton Abbot
Moreton-in-Marsh to Worcester
Newton Abbot to Plymouth
Newbury to Westbury
Oxford to Moreton-in-Marsh
Paddington to Ealing
Paddington to Princes Risborough
Plymouth to St. Austell
Princes Risborough to Banbury
Reading to Didcot
Slough to Newbury
St. Austell to Penzance
Swindon to Bristol
Swindon to Newport
Taunton to Exeter
Westbury to Taunton

MIDLAND MAIN LINES
Bedford to Wellingborough
Euston to Harrow & Wealdstone
Gloucester to Bristol
Harrow to Watford
St. Albans to Bedford
St. Pancras to St. Albans

COUNTRY RAILWAY ROUTES
Abergavenny to Merthyr
Andover to Southampton
Bath to Evercreech Junction
Bath Green Park to Bristol
Bournemouth to Evercreech Junction
Brecon to Newport
Burnham to Evercreech Junction
Cheltenham to Andover
Croydon to East Grinstead
Didcot to Winchester
East Kent Light Railway
Fareham to Salisbury
Frome to Bristol
Guildford to Redhill
Reading to Basingstoke
Reading to Guildford
Redhill to Ashford
Salisbury to Westbury
Stratford upon Avon to Cheltenham
Strood to Paddock Wood
Taunton to Barnstaple
Wenford Bridge to Fowey
Westbury to Bath
Woking to Alton
Yeovil to Dorchester

GREAT RAILWAY ERAS
Ashford from Steam to Eurostar
Festiniog in the Fifties
Festiniog in the Sixties
Festiniog 50 years of enterprise
Isle of Wight Lines 50 years of change
Railways to Victory 1944-46
Return to Blaenau 1970-82
SECR Centenary album
Talyllyn 50 years of change
Wareham to Swanage 50 years of change
Yeovil 50 years of change

LONDON SUBURBAN RLYS
Caterham and Tattenham Corner
Charing Cross to Dartford
Clapham Jn. to Beckenham Jn.
Crystal Palace (HL) & Catford Loop
East London Line
Finsbury Park to Alexandra Palace
Holborn Viaduct to Lewisham
Kingston and Hounslow Loops
Lewisham to Dartford
Lines around Wimbledon
Liverpool Street to Chingford
Mitcham Junction Lines
North London Line
South London Line
West Croydon to Epsom
West London Line
Willesden Junction to Richmond
Wimbledon to Beckenham
Wimbledon to Epsom

STEAMING THROUGH
Steaming through Cornwall
Steaming through the Isle of Wight
Steaming through Kent
Steaming through West Hants

TRAMWAY CLASSICS
Aldgate & Stepney Tramways
Barnet & Finchley Tramways
Bath Tramways
Brighton's Tramways
Bristol's Tramways
Burton & Ashby Tramways
Camberwell & W.Norwood Tramways
Clapham & Streatham Tramways
Croydon's Tramways
Derby Tramways
Dover's Tramways
East Ham & West Ham Tramways
Edgware and Willesden Tramways
Eltham & Woolwich Tramways
Embankment & Waterloo Tramways
Exeter & Taunton Tramways
Fulwell – Home to Trams, Trolleys and Buses
Great Yarmouth Tramways
Greenwich & Dartford Tramways
Hammersmith & Hounslow Tramways
Hampstead & Highgate Tramways
Holborn & Finsbury Tramways
Ilford & Barking Tramways
Kingston & Wimbledon Tramways
Lewisham & Catford Tramways
Liverpool Tramways 1. Eastern Routes
Liverpool Tramways 2. Southern Routes
Liverpool Tramways 3. Northern Routes
Maidstone & Chatham Tramways
Margate to Ramsgate
North Kent Tramways
Norwich Tramways
Reading Tramways
Shepherds Bush & Uxbridge Tramways
Southend-on-sea Tramways
South London Line Tramways 1903-33
Southwark & Deptford Tramways
Stamford Hill Tramways
Twickenham & Kingston Tramways
Victoria & Lambeth Tramways
Waltham Cross & Edmonton Tramways
Walthamstow & Leyton Tramways
Wandsworth & Battersea Tramways

TROLLEYBUS CLASSICS
Bradford Trolleybuses
Croydon Trolleybuses
Darlington Trolleybuses
Derby Trolleybuses
Huddersfield Trolleybuses
Hull Trolleybuses
Portsmouth Trolleybuses
Reading Trolleybuses

WATERWAY & SHIPPING
Kent and East Sussex Waterways
London to Portsmouth Waterway
Sussex Shipping - Sail, Steam & Motor
West Sussex Waterways

MILITARY BOOKS
Battle over Portsmouth
Battle over Sussex 1940
Blitz over Sussex 1941-42
Bombers over Sussex 1943-45
Bognor at War
East Ridings Secret Resistance
Military Defence of West Sussex
Military Signals from the South Coast
Secret Sussex Resistance
Sussex Home Guard
Surrey Home Guard

OTHER RAILWAY BOOKS
Collectors for Trains, Trolleys & Trams
Industrial Railways of the South-East
South Eastern & Chatham Railways
London Chatham & Dover Railways
London Termini - Past and Proposed
War on the Line (SR 1939-45)